To

MRS ORWELL

OBERON BOOKS
LONDON

WWW.OBERONBOOKS.COM

First published in 2017 by Oberon Books Ltd
521 Caledonian Road, London N7 9RH
Tel: +44 (0) 20 7607 3637 / Fax: +44 (0) 20 7607 3629
e-mail: info@oberonbooks.com
www.oberonbooks.com

A catalogue record for this book is available from the British
Library.

PB ISBN: 978-1-78682-265-9
E ISBN: 978-1-78682-266-6

Cover design by Felix Trench

Printed and bound by CPI Group (UK) Ltd, Croydon, CR0 4YY.

Characters

GEORGE ORWELL (46)

SONIA BROWNELL (30)

FRED WARBURG (51)

LUCIAN FREUD (27)

NURSE (40)

Mrs Orwell was first performed at The Old Red Lion, London on 1 August 2017 with the following cast:

SONIA BROWNELL	Cressida Bonas
GEORGE ORWELL	Peter Hamilton Dyer
LUCIEN FREUD	Edmund Digby Jones
FRED WARBURG	Robert Stocks
NURSE	Rosie Ede

Creative Team

Director	Jimmy Walters
Designer	Rebecca Brownell
Composer	Jeremy Warmsley
Lighting Designer	Simon Gethin Thomas
Production Manager	Ned Lay
Stage Manager	Sofie Arnkil
Assistant Director	Piers Sherwood Roberts
Production Assistant	Daisy Blower
Visual Editor	Robert Boulton
Public Relations	Chloe Nelkin Consultants

The Old Red Lion Theatre first opened its doors in 1979 and is now one of London's oldest and most loved Fringe theatre venues.

Our mission is to nurture and present the very best new and emerging theatrical talent. Kathy Burke, Stephen Daldry, Penelope Skinner and Nina Raine are just a few who had early work presented on our stage and this list grows each year.

In the past few years the Old Red Lion Theatre has transferred work off-Broadway and four times to the West End. Notable hits beyond the Fringe include: the World Premiere of Arthur Miller's first play *No Villain* (Trafalgar Studios); *Donkey Heart* (Trafalgar Studios); *The Play That Goes Wrong* (Trafalgar Studios and No 1 Tour); *Mercury Fur* (Trafalgar Studios); *Kissing Sid James* (London and off-Broadway); *The Importance of Being Earnest* (Theatre Royal Haymarket)

Artistic Director: Clive Judd

Executive Director: Damien Devine

General Manager: Helen Devine

Literary Manager: Gus Miller

Bar Manager: Dwaine Strong

September 1949.

SFX: Sound mix of nurses/hospital porter/the clatter of trolleys.

Room 65, University College Hospital, a private room leading on to a corridor with two or three chairs for visitors.

A starchily efficient nurse of indeterminate age looks through the porthole in the door of Room 65, opens it, and crosses to draw the curtains at the window.

Then she crosses to the bed and helps the occupant to sit up.

We now see that the patient, GEORGE ORWELL, is an austerely romantic figure with a narrow clipped moustache and plebeian haircut who looks a bit like Don Quixote, the Knight of the Woeful Countenance.

He starts coughing. The nurse holds a china spittoon to his mouth.

NURSE: How did you sleep?

> *ORWELL makes to tell her but before he can do so, she puts a thermometer in his mouth and reaches for his hand to take his pulse.*

Last night we had snoek. Have you had snoek?

> *ORWELL makes negative sounds through the thermometer in his mouth.*

It's a new South African fish. You'll have seen the posters. They're everywhere. So I got a tin. Quite cheap. One and four. I made us a salad called snoek piquante. From the recipe. There's eight recipes.

> *She takes the thermometer from ORWELL's mouth, looks at it, frowns.*

ORWELL: And what's it like?

NURSE: What?

ORWELL: The snoek.

NURSE: It's horrible. But it's five points less than the salmon.

> *ORWELL has another coughing fit, spitting sputum into the china dish hastily put in place by the nurse.*
>
> *The NURSE, meantime, fills a basin from the tap, puts the basin on the bedside table and folds down ORWELL's sheet to reveal the upper part of his torso. Then, starting with his face, she gives him a blanket bath.*

Still, mustn't grumble, there's always someone worse off than yourself. Though things could be better all round, couldn't they? After all, who won the war?

ORWELL makes to say something just as the nurse wipes his face before making a start on his chest and stomach.

Know what I paid for coal this week? Four and ten. Yes, four and ten. And full of slate and stone at that. And don't talk to me about cigarettes. Three and four a packet of twenty. You heard what Cripps said, I suppose?

ORWELL: No.

NURSE: He said we all need to smoke a bit slower.

ORWELL: Slower?

NURSE: To make the cigarettes last a bit longer. And throw the stubs away a bit shorter. Roll over for me, will you please? He says it would be good for our health. I mean, what's health got to do with it?

The NURSE helps ORWELL roll on to his side.

Saw 'Samson and Delilah' last night. With Hedy Lamarr and Victor Mature.

ORWELL: Which part did he play?

NURSE: Why, Samson, of course. My friend Lettie is crazy about him. Well, he looks so holy, doesn't he? Do you like going to the pictures at all?

ORWELL: No.

NURSE: Why ever not?

ORWELL: I used to be a film critic.

NURSE: Oh.

The NURSE folds the sheet back over ORWELL, empties the basin and returns to the bedside.

Now how about a nice cup of tea?

ORWELL: You use a pot, do you?

NURSE: Can't make tea without a pot.

ORWELL: And how big is this pot?

The NURSE uses her hands to indicate a pot of medium size.

China, is it? Or earthenware?

ORWELL reaches across to the bedside cabinet and produces a packet of tea.

And I want you to use this tea, if you please, and be generous. I mean, don't fret about the coupons, put in six or seven heaped teaspoons and don't stir it if you please – just, you know, swirl it around a bit. And help yourself to a peach, why don't you?

The NURSE has been unable to keep her eyes from straying to a box of fresh peaches on a side table. Now she takes a peach from the box and puts it in her pocket.

Take two. They'll make a nice change to the snoek.

The NURSE takes another peach and turns to exit, almost bumping into FREDRIC WARBURG, a 51 year old publisher who walks down the hospital corridor and opens the door of Room 65.

He, too, spies the peaches.

WARBURG: Where did you get these?

ORWELL: David Astor. They were here when we arrived.

WARBURG: We?

ORWELL: Sonia came in the ambulance with me.

WARBURG: Has Morland been in to see you yet?

ORWELL: No.

WARBURG: Well, you'll find him a first class man. He looked after Pamela's first husband, you know.

ORWELL: Were they divorced?

WARBURG: No, the poor chap died. But I can assure you that Morland has a first class reputation and a keen understanding of creative types. He took charge of D. H. Lawrence.

ORWELL gives WARBURG a knowing look.

The NURSE enters with a pot of tea, cup and saucer, milk jug, sugar bowl on tray.

NURSE: Twenty minutes. Mr Morland was most specific.

WARBURG waves the NURSE out of the room. NURSE exits, offended. WARBURG pours ORWELL a cup of tea.

ORWELL: Tea in first if you please.

WARBURG: Very well.

ORWELL: If you pour the tea in first, you see, you can more precisely regulate the amount of milk that goes in, whereas, if you do it the other way round, you're liable to put in too much milk.

WARBURG: Sugar?

ORWELL: Absolutely not. One might just as well put in pepper or salt.

ORWELL pours the tea from his cup into the saucer and drinks it with a loud sucking noise.

WARBURG: Anyway, I have good news.

WARBURG opens his briefcase and produces a first edition of '1984'.

Last night I got a call from New York.

ORWELL: Yes?

WARBURG: It was from the Book-of-the-Month Club. Yes, the Book-of-the-Month Club, George. Think of the sales. The royalties.

ORWELL: Much good may they do me in here.

WARBURG: You won't be in here forever, George.

ORWELL: But look at me, Fred.

WARBURG: It's the streptomycin, George.

ORWELL: I'm not on streptomycin now.

WARBURG: And that's why you're looking so much better.

ORWELL picks up a bedside mirror and examines his face.

You are a much loved writer, George, and your public wants you to get well. That's why we insisted you come here. To a first-class man like Morland. Now let's talk about this marvellous news.

ORWELL: What news?

WARBURG: The Book-of-the-Month Club, George. They have a couple of suggestions.

ORWELL: Have they indeed?

WARBURG: They want you to cut the Appendix on Newspeak.

ORWELL: Say again.

WARBURG: The committee…

ORWELL: The committee?

WARBURG: Of the American Book-of-the-Month Club. They want you to cut the Appendix.

ORWELL: No.

WARBURG: No?

ORWELL: A book, Fred, as you well know, is built up of a balanced structure and one simply cannot remove chunks here and there unless one is ready to recast the whole thing.

WARBURG: But think about the money, George.

ORWELL: You think about the money, Fred. Leave me to think about the book.

WARBURG: So what shall I tell them?

ORWELL: Tell them no.

WARBURG: I beg you to think it over, George.

ORWELL: I have thought it over.

The NURSE enters with a breakfast tray.

NURSE: Now you eat up some of this breakfast for me. That's butter, you know, not margarine.

ORWELL: Thank you, nurse.

NURSE exits.

ORWELL tentatively picks up a slice of toast and reluctantly takes a bite.

This precipitates a coughing fit and he waves a hand at the china basin that WARBURG gives him to catch the sputum.

Once the coughing fit is over ORWELL leans back against his pillows and reaches out for tobacco and papers with which he expertly rolls a cigarette, lights it, sighs happily.

WARBURG crosses to the window and looks out.

See any Rolls-Royces?

WARBURG: What's that, George?

ORWELL: Rolls-Royces. Out there. In the street.

WARBURG: Not many, no.

ORWELL: There shouldn't be any. Not under a Labour government.

WARBURG: They mostly belong to foreigners.

ORWELL: Is that a fact?

WARBURG: And then there's the Embassy cars, of course.

ORWELL: Well, they should be banned. It's bad for morale, one class being visibly better off.

WARBURG wanders about the room, taking in two easy chairs, a commode and a bottle of whisky.

ORWELL: Help yourself to a Scotch.

WARBURG looks at his watch, but then succumbs.

WARBURG: Will you have one? Help settle that cough.

ORWELL: Yes, rightyho.

WARBURG pours two glasses of whisky and hands one to ORWELL, who lifts the glass up to his nose.

That's Jura peat and the tang of salt air. I'd give my right arm to be there right now.

WARBURG: But not your right lung, I assume? Who's looking after the place in your absence?

ORWELL: My sister Avril. And her bloke.

WARBURG: Is he a good chap?

ORWELL: I certainly hope so. He's lending Avril a hand with Richard.

WARBURG: Miss him?

ORWELL: Well, of course I miss him. How can you ask?

WARBURG: Well, our fathers didn't seem to miss us.

ORWELL: But I brought Richard up on my own and we've become the best of pals. I suppose that's why I miss him so much.

ORWELL succumbs to a coughing fit. WARBURG hands him the china basin. ORWELL spits up phlegm, takes a drink of whisky. WARBURG makes to put the basin away.

Leave it out, Fred, if you please. They have to boil all the china, you see.

WARBURG looks at the contents of the china bowl and puts it down on an open surface.

SONIA BROWNELL walks down the hospital corridor and opens the door to Room 65.

She immediately crosses to the bed and removes ORWELL's glass of whisky.

ORWELL: Oh, hello Sonia.

WARBURG sees that SONIA is not best pleased, looks at his glass of whisky, finishes it, puts the glass back on the table, picks up his homburg and briefcase and makes to leave.

WARBURG: Book-of-the-Month Club, George.

ORWELL: What about it?

WARBURG: Talk some sense into him, Sonia.

SONIA: That may prove beyond even me.

WARBURG exits.

SONIA makes to kiss ORWELL, thinks better of it and holds his hand.

We now see that she looks like one of Renoir's pink-flushed girls, except that her stare is both more provocative and more guarded.

She is, however, demurely dressed in a plain dark skirt and sweater over a lace-collared white blouse.

She pulls up a chair, sits beside ORWELL's bed, opens her briefcase, sorts through some papers and hands ORWELL an envelope.

SONIA: This came for you.

ORWELL takes the letter, turns it over.

ORWELL: 10 Downing Street?

SONIA: Yes.

ORWELL opens the letter, reads.

ORWELL: It's from the Prime Minister. Someone must have said I was dying.

SONIA: But you're not dying.

ORWELL: Well, Attlee certainly thinks I am. Why else would he write to wish me well? Have you met Attlee?

SONIA: No, George, I haven't. What's he like?

ORWELL: Like a dead fish before it's stiffened.

SONIA sorts through the rest of ORWELL's correspondence, her movements both rapid and incisive, with everything reinforced by flashing smiles, emphatic nods, expressive hand movements and the dramatic flinging back of ash blonde hair through which she runs her fingers to disarrange, rearrange or twist into shapes.

SONIA: These are from various publications all chasing you up for pieces you must have promised them. 'Atlantic Monthly', 'Time and Tide', 'Tribune'. I've sent back the usual response telling them you're seriously ill and unable to meet the deadline.

ORWELL: Good.

SONIA: And this is from your American agent. Wants to know if this is an acceptable sum for translation rights.

ORWELL: Where?

SONIA: Argentina.

ORWELL: I've no idea, have you?

SONIA: Not a clue. So I'll tell him it sounds alright, shall I?

ORWELL: Yes.

SONIA: But then he bangs on about censorship and whether you're prepared to make cuts. I've said under no circumstance.

She picks up the book on ORWELL's bedside table.

What's this you're reading?

ORWELL: Somerset Maugham. I think he's absolutely first class. Here, listen to this. 'Death ends all things…'

SONIA: Oh, George, don't.

ORWELL: No, listen, listen. 'Death ends all things and so is the comprehensive conclusion of a story, but marriage finishes it very properly too and the sophisticated are ill-advised to sneer at what is by convention termed a happy ending.'

ORWELL reaches a hand out to SONIA. SONIA holds ORWELL's hand very briefly, lets it go.

ORWELL: Please.

SONIA: What?

ORWELL: Give me your hand.

ORWELL again holds out his hand, SONIA takes it, helps ORWELL on to his feet and into a bulky fawn cardigan.

ORWELL: What time tomorrow?

SONIA: Bit hard to tell, with Cyril away.

ORWELL: Well, you know, whenever.

SONIA closes the door and exits down the hospital corridor.

Light from the window changes to indicate passage of time.

SFX: Sound mix of trolley bus/charladies/'Workers' Playtime' radio show.

ORWELL, wrapped in his bulky fawn cardigan, sits in an easy chair opposite WARBURG.

Both are reading newspapers.

'A two-bar electric fire needlesslyswitched on for 20 minutes robs the country of one pound of coal urgently needed to bring recovery to us all.' Well, I object to these attempts by the government to insinuate a sense of sin among working class people. And, to cap it all, look at this.

ORWELL passes WARBURG the paper.

WARBURG: What is it I'm meant to be looking at?

ORWELL: That advertisement there.

WARBURG: What's wrong with it?

ORWELL: What do you mean what's wrong with it? What's wrong with it Fred, is that they've taken the winged god Mercury and put him in a pair of underpants.

WARBURG: Quite comical, what?

ORWELL: Well, I've nothing against blasphemy but damn it all this chap's a paen to physical beauty. He should be shielded from this vulgar nonsense.

WARBURG: And how might you go about that?

ORWELL: I'd ban it.

WARBURG: Really?

ORWELL: Yes I would. Then I'd hunt down the advertising wallahs responsible and shoot them.

WARBURG: I thought I'd find you in a better frame of mind.

ORWELL: Why?

WARBURG: Well, Morland seems very pleased with you.

ORWELL: He won't let me do any writing though, will he?

WARBURG: Not straight away no.

ORWELL: But you know better than I do, Fred, that no writer lasts forever, even in good health. He has an initial impulse for what, three or four books? But sooner or later he runs out of steam. And another thing.

WARBURG: What?

ORWELL: I can't stand the thought of being sedentary. I like chopping wood and all that. The last time I was on Jura I could hardly pull a weed without running a temperature.

WARBURG: You know what you need, don't you, George?

ORWELL: What?

WARBURG: You need the love of a good woman.

ORWELL: Have you anyone in mind?

WARBURG: Well, I thought you had a fancy for Sonia.

ORWELL: And who hasn't got a fancy for Sonia? People go into 'Horizon' just so they can look at her.

WARBURG: She's bright as a button.

ORWELL: No doubt about that.

WARBURG: She's a very efficient editor.

ORWELL: True.

WARBURG: She could handle your literary affairs.

ORWELL: But what can I offer a woman like Sonia?

WARBURG: Well, I need scarcely remind you, George, that soon you will be a very rich man.

ORWELL: Oh, Sonia doesn't care about money. Besides, she can have any man she wants.

WARBURG: With the exception of Maurice Ponty.

ORWELL: Really? How do you know this?

WARBURG: Well, I keep my ear to the ground. Anyway, what I'm saying, George, is that if some french johnny has broken her heart this might be a good time to step in.

ORWELL: You think so?

WARBURG: I do. I mean time is not on her side.

ORWELL: It's not on mine either. 44.

WARBURG: What?

ORWELL: 44. That's the age Anton Chekhov died. As did Robert Louis Stevenson and D. H. Lawrence. 44.

WARBURG: And you are?

ORWELL: 46.

WARBURG: Well, there you are. See what giant strides we've made. And you, my friend, have years in you, provided you look after yourself. Or, better still, find someone to look after you.

Light from the window again indicates the passage of time.

SFX: Sound mix made up of typewriter keys/clippie on bus/news vendor shouting 'Star, News, or Evening Standard'.

ORWELL sits in a chair with SONIA beside him, she in dark skirt and blouse, he in bulky fawn cardigan, bedroom slippers.

She hands him a letter.

SONIA: Harcourt Price wants to put together an American edition of your essays. What do you say to that?

ORWELL: Well, I don't want 'How The Poor Die' reprinted. Nor 'Bookshop Memories' or 'Spilling The Beans'. They were written when Eileen and I were starving. I think I got ten quid a pop.

SONIA: Then there's a rather odd one here from some emigre group who promise to circulate copies of 'Nineteen Eighty Four' throughout Russia if you'll forego the translation fee.

ORWELL reads the emigre group's letter in silence.

ORWELL: Can you make dumplings?

SONIA: I've never tried.

ORWELL: Think you might learn to make dumplings, though?

SONIA: Oh, I should think so. If I tried.

ORWELL: And do you think you'd be willing to try?

SONIA: I might, George, I might.

ORWELL: That's settled then.

SONIA: What is?

ORWELL: Well, our getting married, of course.

SONIA: Was that a proposal?

ORWELL: Yes, it was.

SONIA: I don't love you, you know.

ORWELL: Well, of course you don't.

SONIA: Then why would you want to marry me?

ORWELL: Because I'll get better. I've got to get better, you see, because other considerations aside, I have a great idea for a novel.

SONIA: And that's why you want to marry me?

ORWELL: Well, there's nothing really in my life aside from my work and seeing that Richard gets a good start. I realize it's absurd, of course, a person like me asking someone like you and I wouldn't be offended, or ever hurt, if you simply say no. I mean I'm a good fifteen...

SONIA: Sixteen.

ORWELL: ...years older than you but I do so want someone to share what's left of my life and my work.

ORWELL stands to pace the room, revealing at once how clumsy he is, how prone to tripping over things or knocking things over.

I know you don't love me. Well, how could you? I mean, you are young and fresh and you've had someone you really loved and who has set up a standard I couldn't compete with. I'm talking about that French chappie now, the philosopher.

SONIA: Maurice.

ORWELL: Yes, Maurice. Well, obviously I can't compete with him. And if you want a handsome young man who can give you lots of children, then I'm not the man for you. On the other hand, if you want children by someone else it wouldn't bother me very much.

SONIA: Really?

ORWELL: Well, I've little physical jealousy, and you are so young and beautiful you deserve somebody better than me. On the other hand, if you don't find such a person you could do worse, supposing, that is, I'm not actually disgusting to you. What I'm really asking you is whether you would like to be the widow of a literary man. I mean, you'd get royalties coming in and so forth and you might even find it interesting to edit my unpublished stuff. Of course there's no knowing how long I'll live. I mean, I've been supposed to die several times, but I always lived on just to spite them. Ideally, I'd like to live another ten years because I think I have another three worthwhile books in me. Oh, Sonia, you are my only hope.

ORWELL falls to his knees in front of her. She runs her fingers through his hair, then turns towards the window.

SONIA: So what you want, in a nutshell, George, is a mistress, housekeeper, nurse, literary executor and mother for Richard?

ORWELL: Yes.

SONIA: Well, no doubt that's all very sensible of you.

ORWELL: Yes.

SONIA: And I'm sure there's some literary lass out there who will see it as her mission in life to look after both you and your son. It is, however, an offer that makes little appeal to me.

ORWELL: She will also, of course, inherit a sizeable income.

SONIA: Are you trying to woo me, George?

ORWELL: Yes.

SONIA: Well, you're making a very poor job of it.

ORWELL: I'm not very good with women, Sonia.

SONIA: Is that a fact?

ORWELL: Women don't like men very much, do they?

SONIA: Where on earth did you get that idea?

ORWELL: From my mother, I suppose.

SONIA: Why? What did she say?

ORWELL: Well, I got the distinct impression that she looked up on man as a sort of large smelly animal who forced his attentions on women.

SONIA: What, sexually?

ORWELL: Yes.

SONIA: Well, let me tell you she's wrong on that score.

ORWELL: Anyway, what a bore it is. Whycan't we be like animals, minutes of ferocious lust and months of icy chastity?

SONIA: And that's your recipe for a successful marriage, is it?

ORWELL: Well, up to a point, yes. I mean, what with the illness and all that, I'm pretty much impotent anyway and I thought that might appeal to you. What I want, Sonia, is a wife.

NURSE enters with tea tray.

NURSE: Why, Mr Orwell, you look quite unwell. Has Miss Brownell been taxing your strength?

SONIA: Believe me, nurse, if I'd been taxing his strength, he'd know it.

Once again the light source from the window indicates a passage of time.

SFX: Sound mix of ITMA/cockney gossip/ticket collector.

ORWELL sits up in bed while the 28 year old LUCIAN FREUD draws his portrait.

FREUD has voluptuous lips, a head of dark curls and eyes that dart from side to side like fleas in a snuffbox.

But, while he generates an intense nervous energy, his speech is quite tortured because of his German-inflected accent and rolling 'r's.

Now FREUD breaks off from his drawing and puts his fingers on ORWELL's neck.

FREUD: What happened here?

ORWELL: I was shot.

FREUD: Who by?

ORWELL: A fascist sniper.

FREUD: When?

ORWELL: In the Spanish Civil War. A great many of my friends were killed and others simply disappeared.

FREUD: You were lucky then.

ORWELL: That's certainly how I felt at the time. Now I'm not sure. I think on balance it's better to die violently and not too old. I mean, we talk about the horror of war, but what weapon has man invented that even approaches the cruelty of a common disease like mine. Natural death, as you can see, is slow, smelly and painful.

For a while all that can be heard is the sound of FREUD's charcoal on paper.

Know what shocked me coming back to England? All these intellectuals writing poems about 'necessary murder', justifying the purges and so on. Playing with fire, the lot of them, without even knowing the fire was hot.

FREUD: But I take it you're still a Socialist?

ORWELL: Yes. But God, how I hate them. They're so priggish, aren't they? So dictatorial. So freakish.

FREUD: In what way?

ORWELL: In the way they all flock to the smell of 'progress' like bluebottles to a dead cat. The soul-savers and the Nosey Parkers, the fruit-juice drinkers, the sandal-wearers, the pacifists, the feminists. Sorry, Lucian, got carried away.

FREUD: In any event, I disagree.

ORWELL: Really?

FREUD: I think England is a marvellous place, and if you were a German Jew, so would you.

ORWELL: Well, at least we don't kill each other, I suppose. On the other hand, our national emblem is a bulldog, an animal noted for its ugliness and impenetrable stupidity. How old were you when you got here?

FREUD: Ten.

ORWELL: So you were schooled here?

FREUD: You could say that. I was sent to Dartington Hall.

ORWELL: The free school?

FREUD: Yes.

ORWELL: I thought they let you do what you like.

FREUD: They do. But what I liked to do was fight people.

ORWELL: Why?

FREUD: I didn't understand what they were saying, so I hit them. It's very hard to make friends that way.

ORWELL: And where did you go after that?

FREUD: Bryanston. I was expelled from Bryanston too.

ORWELL: Why?

FREUD: They said I was a disruptive influence.

ORWELL: And were you?

FREUD: I suppose I was.

ORWELL: Why? What did you do?

FREUD: Dropped my trousers.

ORWELL: Where?

FREUD: Bournemouth.

ORWELL: Oh.

FREUD: Then I met Stephen. Stephen Spender. He published a drawing of mine in 'Horizon'. I think that must be where you and I met.

A period of intense concentration by FREUD in which nothing can be heard but the working of FREUD's pencil on paper.

ORWELL: Where are you living nowadays?

FREUD: Delamere Terrace in Paddington.

ORWELL: And what's that like?

FREUD: It's an absolute dump, but it's got this very shabby light that appeals to me more than Paris.

ORWELL: You've lived in Paris?

FREUD: Yes, I have.

ORWELL: Did you meet Picasso?

FREUD: Yes.

ORWELL: What's he like?

FREUD: He's very small. He complains that in London men's trousers are up to here.

FREUD draws a line across his chin.

I think that's why his nudes are so massive. He showed me some of his paintings once and asked me to choose the ones I liked best. I picked out four or five of them and he said 'I'm pleased you've chosen those as they're some I painted yesterday.' But when I touched them the paint was quite dry. I don't really think he's a very nice man. In fact, I think he's poisonous. Not that it matters either way.

ORWELL: Have you met Dali?

FREUD: No, have you?

ORWELL: Yes.

FREUD: What's he like?

ORWELL: He's an absolute shit.

FREUD: All artists are.

ORWELL: Including yourself?

FREUD: Oh, yes, I'm an absolute shit.

Long period of intense concentration by FREUD, interrupted occasionally by him talking to himself. He fiddles with the curtain to adjust the light.

ORWELL: What's the weather like out there?

FREUD: It's cold.

ORWELL: If I was at home on Jura today I'd stand a good chance of seeing an eagle.

FREUD: I have a kestrel.

ORWELL: Where?

FREUD: At home.

ORWELL: In Paddington?

FREUD: Yes, I have it trained to land on my wrist.

ORWELL: But how do you feed it?

FREUD: I shoot rats on the Regent's Canal.

ORWELL: With what?

FREUD: A Luger.

ORWELL: Don't people object?

FREUD: No, I don't think so. My neighbours are all criminals.

ORWELL: Really?

FREUD: The man in the flat downstairs from me is supposed to have killed someone. But the night he did it he was with me. At least that's what I told the police.

ORWELL: Did they believe you?

FREUD: No, not at all. They hauled me in for questioning. But later that night I went dancing with Princess Margaret.

ORWELL says nothing but is clearly intrigued.

Well, there was a photograph in the papers. Police left us both alone after that.

FREUD returns to extreme concentration on the job in hand.

Do you know what I like about art?

ORWELL: What?

FREUD: The risk. I mean half the point of doing a drawing is not knowing how it's going to turn out. If I did know I wouldn't bother doing it. Then often when a piece is finished I don't like it anyway.

ORWELL: So what do you do?

19

FREUD: I destroy it.

ORWELL: It's all ego, you know, this creative stuff, a desire to be remembered. When you're dead.

FREUD: On the door outside it says 'Eric Blair'.

ORWELL: So?

FREUD: So why be remembered as somebody else?

ORWELL: Well, my parents were ashamed of me, what with all that 'down and out' stuff.

FREUD: But why choose 'George Orwell?'

ORWELL: I usually say it's 'George' for the king and 'Orwell' for the river in Suffolk, but I changed my name because of the bookshops. Imagine you're in a book shop, see? If you're name's at the front of the alphabet, your books are stuck on the top on the left. If your name's at the other end, your books will be somewhere down there at your feet. But 'Orwell', starting with an 'O', is always slap-bang in the middle. Secret of my success.

FREUD: Is that true?

ORWELL: No, total lie.

SONIA enters, taken aback to see FREUD in the room.

Oh, hello Sonia.

SONIA: Lu, what on earth are you doing here?

FREUD: I should have thought that was obvious.

SONIA: How long has he been here, George?

ORWELL: I don't know, an hour or so.

SONIA: Well, that is just ridiculous. And you, Lucian, should know better. Look at him, the man is exhausted.

ORWELL: Bunk.

SONIA: Allow me to know best, please George.

FREUD looks at the half finished drawing.

FREUD: It looks like I shall have to come back.

FREUD puts his pad and pencils away and starts to put on the fur-collared great coat that has hung on the back of the door, obliterating the porthole window.

SONIA: Well, just make sure you ask me first.

ORWELL: That really is a marvellous coat.

FREUD: Yes, it was my grandfather's.

ORWELL: Did you draw him?

FREUD: No. Well, he had this sort of hole in his face, like a brown apple. I think that's why there wasn't a death mask.

SONIA: On that note…

FREUD: Yes.

SONIA: I'll see you out.

They exit, closing the door behind them and they confront each other in the hospital corridor.

FREUD: Why are you wearing all that makeup? You know I hate women smeared in makeup. You can never see who they are.

SONIA: You don't mind Francis wearing makeup.

FREUD: Francis, Sonia, is an artist. You've only to see him mix bootpolish.

SONIA: And what am I?

FREUD: Well, frankly I'm beginning to wonder.

SONIA: Oh, fuck off, Lucian.

FREUD: Sonia, you must listen to me. George is a wonderful chap, a great artist and all that, but you must face facts, he's going to die.

SONIA: He's not going to die! He's not going to die! I can save him, I know I can save him. And George knows I can save him too. That's why I'm going to marry him, so that he will survive and write wonderful books.

FREUD: You're marrying George?

SONIA: Yes, I'm marrying George.

FREUD: Say it again.

SONIA: I'm marrying George.

FREUD: Well, I'm sure you'll be very happy together.

SONIA: You might sound a little more convinced. Hey, where are you going?

FREUD: To say well done to George, of course.

SONIA: You can't do that.

FREUD: Why?

SONIA: I haven't actually told him yet.

FREUD: Oh.

SONIA returns to Room 65, leaving a bemused FREUD to exit.

ORWELL: Is that a good looking man, would you say?

SONIA: Lucian? God, the man is feral.

ORWELL: He goes dancing with Princess Margaret.

SONIA: Well, that's not a feather in his cap. I mean, have you seen her? The woman's a pygmy.

ORWELL: Is he married? I can't tell.

SONIA: I don't know that anybody can.

ORWELL: And yet he's devoted to his work. Where on earth does he find the time?

SONIA: Well, it's all he does, George. Paint and chase women.

ORWELL: Yes, that must be it.

SONIA walks up and down, distracted.

SONIA: What do you see in him anyway?

ORWELL: Well, Freud has got something I've always wanted.

SONIA: And what's that?

ORWELL: To be irresistible to women.

SONIA: Really? What a lowly desire.

ORWELL: It comes of being unattractive, you see.

SONIA: You're not unattractive, George, you're just very serious.

ORWELL: You make it sound like an accusation.

SONIA: Well, you can't have a fling with a serious man.

ORWELL: Why?

SONIA: Because you always get involved.

ORWELL: And women don't want to get involved?

SONIA: Well, if you're going to get involved you might as well get married, and lots of girls don't want to get married.

ORWELL: What do they want then?

SONIA: They want to have fun.

ORWELL: Well, I'm no good at having fun.

SONIA: No, that's why they call you Gloomy George.

ORWELL: And who calls me Gloomy George?

SONIA: Oh, everyone.

ORWELL: And that's why you're turning me down, I suppose?

SONIA: I don't believe I've turned you down.

ORWELL: Really?

SONIA: Yes, really.

ORWELL: Well, you're not leaping up and down either.

SONIA: I've been through an awful lot, George, what with one thing and another. And marriage is a very big step.

ORWELL: But you're willing to entertain the thought?

SONIA: Yes, George, I am.

ORWELL: Oh, Sonia, you've made me so very happy.

SONIA: I didn't say yes, George.

Light source from the window changes to denote passage of time.

SFX: Sound mix of news bulletin/popular song/nurse's chatter.

NURSE attends to ORWELL's bed bath while, in the hospital corridor, SONIA waits to see him.

WARBURG walks down corridor, tips his hat to SONIA.

WARBURG: Good morning, Sonia.

SONIA: Hello Fred. What brings you here?

WARBURG: I wanted to bring George up to date.

SONIA: With what?

WARBURG: A few things on the business front.

SONIA: He's asked me to deal with those.

WARBURG: But this involves finance.

SONIA: You can speak quite freely to me, Fred.

WARBURG: Can I?

SONIA: Yes.

WARBURG opens his briefcase and hands SONIA a sheaf of paper.

And what does this mean?

WARBURG takes the paper back.

WARBURG: It means, Sonia, that '1984' will make George even more money than 'Animal Farm'. To date we have sold 22,700 copies and are now preparing another edition. Even better news is that the American Book-of-the-Month Club have acceded to George's demand that it be published without any cuts.

SONIA: Well, that's very nice for him.

WARBURG: George loves you very much, you know.

SONIA: I know he does.

WARBURG: And he's a great writer.

SONIA: I know that, Fred.

WARBURG: Maybe he still has some books in him. And when he dies, as one day he must, you will be left a wealthy widow.

There follows a long pause during which WARBURG takes his time re-organising his briefcase.

SONIA: How much?

WARBURG: How much?

SONIA: Yes, Fred, how much?

WARBURG: Well, from British and American rights, digests, translations and foreign rights, um…

SONIA: Put a number on it, Fred.

WARBURG: You'd be looking at…

SONIA: What?

WARBURG: Fifteen thousand a year.

SONIA sits on one of the visitors chairs, staring into space. WARBURG exits.

The NURSE in Room 65 puts the finishing touches to ORWELL's bed bath and 'tips' the bed so that his head is lower than his feet. She exits the room and enters the corridor.

NURSE: Miss Brownell.

SONIA: Nurse.

NURSE: Are you alright, miss? You look rather pale.

SONIA: Yes, I'm fine, I'm fine. How's George?

NURSE: Unwell. So Mr Morland said I should tip him, try and get the phlegm off his chest.

SONIA: Yes.

NURSE: Well, I'll be off. I've got my friend Lettie coming tonight.

SONIA: Well, that will be very nice for you.

NURSE: Have you tried Irish Potato Pancakes?

SONIA: No, not yet. Not ever, in fact.

NURSE: Only I think I'll give them a go.

SONIA opens her handbag and holds out some coupons.

SONIA: Would you like some coupons, nurse?

NURSE: I couldn't do that.

SONIA: Here, take them, please. I'm going to the Cafe Royale tonight. With Jean-Paul Sartre and Simone de Beauvoir.

NURSE is at a loss as to how to take this and covers her confusion in a welter of thanks for the coupons.

25

NURSE: Thank you very much, Miss Brownell. Yes. Thank you very much indeed.

NURSE exits along corridor.

Light source from the window in ORWELL's room changes to denote the passage of time.

SFX: Sound mix of Third Programme/milk bottles on doorstep/MP on hustings.

ORWELL, wrapped in a beige cardigan, sits in an easy chair reading a magazine.

SONIA sits opposite, fiddling.

ORWELL: Bloody Yanks!

SONIA: What have they done now?

ORWELL: They've come up with all these gadgets.

He shows her the magazine.

SONIA: They're labour-saving.

ORWELL: That's it exactly, labour saving. Well, I think the more gadgets women have, and the more they're encouraged to think about their faces and figures, the less they'll want to bring up families. I mean, just look at this underwear. Scanty panties! Scanty panties! Women who think about scanty panties will never have a fire in the fireplace, or a baby in the house, or a dog, or a cat. What are you doing?

SONIA pulls her dress up to reveal her underwear.

SONIA: I'm showing you my scanty panties. There, not quite so bad now, are they, George?

SONIA puts her other hand on GEORGE's nether regions.

If only there was a fire in the fireplace.

SONIA smooths down her dress, goes across to the mirror, combs her hair and puts on makeup.

ORWELL: You're not going?

SONIA: Yes, of course I'm going.

ORWELL: Where?

SONIA: Cocktail party.

ORWELL: Will you be back?

SONIA: No, of course I won't. I mean, Robert and Janetta will be there and so will Lucian and Anne Dunn so we're bound to push on afterwards.

ORWELL: Yes.

NURSE enters with a tray.

SONIA: Oh, I'll take that, nurse.

SONIA takes the tray from NURSE.

Yes, that will be all.

NURSE exits the room. SONIA puts table in front of ORWELL's chair, puts the tray on the table.

Now what have we here?

SONIA removes the lid that covers the plate.

Mmm, Victory pie.

She hands GEORGE his knife and fork and starts to put on her gloves.

You know, George, I really envy you. You're waited on hand and foot in here, and there's always someone at your beck and call.

SONIA kisses GEORGE on the top of the head.

Now see that you get a good night's rest, and don't worry about what I'm up to. I shan't be late. I've a vicious day in the office tomorrow soothing Cyril's troubled brow.

ORWELL: He's back?

SONIA: Yes, and needing his nappy changed.

She checks her appearance one last time and turns to the door, opens it, ducks back inside the room.

And by the way.

ORWELL: Yes?

SONIA: Yes.

ORWELL: What?

SONIA: Yes, I will marry you.

SONIA exits Room 65 and swings off down the corridor leaving ORWELL dazed and confused.

Light source from the window again indicates the passage of time.

SFX: Sound mix of comedian/charladies/classical music.

NURSE is in Room 65 with ORWELL.

WARBURG waits outside ORWELL's room, reading a copy of 'Horizon'.

SONIA walks down hospital corridor towards WARBURG who throws his hands out to her.

WARBURG: Sonia, how lovely to see you, and looking even more radiant than ever.

WARBURG kisses SONIA on the cheek and admires her engagement ring.

And this, my dear, is quite beautiful.

SONIA: Well, thank you, Fred.

WARBURG: Sonia, my heartfelt congratulations. This is the most wonderful news. George certainly needs some loving care.

The door to Room 65 opens. NURSE exits along corridor.

SONIA: And I intend to provide it.

WARBURG: Good girl.

WARBURG makes to follow SONIA into Room 65, SONIA waylays him.

SONIA: I need to be alone with him, Fred. You don't mind, do you?

WARBURG: Of course not, my dear.

SONIA opens the door to Room 65, goes inside. WARBURG watches briefly at the porthole window, smiles to himself, then exits.

SONIA, agitated, paces up and down.

ORWELL: Is something the matter?

SONIA: Yes, George, there is.

ORWELL: You've changed your mind?

SONIA: Worse.

ORWELL: There is nothing worse.

SONIA produces a copy of the 'Evening Standard' from her bag.

SONIA: You haven't seen this.

ORWELL: What is that?

SONIA: The 'Evening Standard'.

ORWELL: Well, what does it say?

SONIA, still standing, takes a deep breath and reads out the article from the 'Evening Standard'.

SONIA: 'A specialist's verdict will decide whether fair-haired Miss Sonia Brownell, engaged to novelist, George Orwell, will have a bedside marriage.'

ORWELL: What?

SONIA: There, I knew you'd be upset.

ORWELL: Well, I am just rather surprised. I mean where do they get hold of this stuff?

SONIA: 'Miss Brownell told me today: 'If the doctors say he is well enough we shall be married within a few weeks."

ORWELL: Did you really say that?

SONIA: Yes I did. I'm sorry, George.

ORWELL: But how did it happen?

SONIA: Well, this reporter came waltzing in, said all of Fleet Street was talking about it, and they'd be printing it anyway.

She hands ORWELL the newspaper.

ORWELL: 'In her Bedford Square office today 30-year-old Miss Brownell, assistant editor of the literary magazine 'Horizon', was wearing an Italian engagement ring of ornamental design with rubies, diamonds and an emerald. She had chosen it herself because she thought it pretty. Her hope is that her husband-to-be, his real name is Eric Blair, will be well enough to leave hospital so that they can go abroad early in the new year.'

SONIA: Oh, George, I'm so sorry. Please forgive me.

ORWELL beckons her to him. SONIA sits on the bed.

ORWELL: There is nothing to forgive.

SONIA: Really?

ORWELL: Sonia, you are my one true love.

SONIA: Well, now that things are out in the open I think we should set a date.

ORWELL: For what?

SONIA: The wedding. And if I'm expected to save your life I think we'd best get married smartish.

ORWELL: Really?

SONIA: Why not? Let's go for November.

ORWELL: But that's next month.

SONIA: No time like the present, George. And let's go for a day no one else would choose. Let's get married on the 13th.

ORWELL: The 13th of November it is. Well, I don't know about you, but I feel positively excited.

SONIA: Are you allowed to get excited? I mean, what would Morland say?

ORWELL: I'm sure he'd say a little excitement might be very good for one. I've never forgotten that night, you know, when you came round to babysit.

SONIA: Well, you were rather more spry at the time.

ORWELL: Yes, wasn't I?

SONIA: And who's to say, if you're well looked after, you might not be spry again one day.

ORWELL: Know what I love about my Sonia?

SONIA: My kindness, my goodness, my strength?

ORWELL: Yes, all that.

SONIA: My beauty?

ORWELL: Of course.

SONIA: My body?

ORWELL: Oh yes.

SONIA: My sex?

ORWELL: Oh yes. But more than that, it's your simple animal desire.

SONIA: Now to the practicalities.

ORWELL: Yes, that's my Sonia.

SONIA: If I'm to look after you properly I shall have to leave my job. I don't envisage it being a problem. Cyril hardly ever turns up and when he does it bores him witless. In fact, Horizon is on its last legs.

SONIA busies herself in preparation to leave.

ORWELL: You're not going, are you?

SONIA: Yes, of course.

ORWELL: Where?

SONIA: To sort out the marriage licence.

ORWELL: And why's that so urgent?

SONIA: Well, we'll have to get married in hospital and the law's a bit sticky about that.

ORWELL: Why?

SONIA: Dying millionaires, designing nurses. We'll need to get a special licence.

ORWELL: And how does one go about that?

SONIA: I've already got it in hand.

ORWELL: Oh.

SONIA: Just one more thing.

ORWELL: Yes.

SONIA: I'm not going to marry you looking like that.

ORWELL: And who would you like me to look like?

SONIA: Someone with a bit more panache.

The light from the window indicates the passage of time.

SFX: Sound mix of wedding march/vows/party atmos.

ORWELL, a huge smile on his face, is dressed in a red velvet smoking jacket and looks unexpectedly grand and military, as if he'd pursued his career in Burma to a successful end.

SONIA stands beside him.

The hospital chaplain, his back to audience, conducts an Anglican wedding service.

ORWELL: I, Eric Arthur Blair, take thee, Sonia Mary, to be my wedded wife, to have and to hold from this day forward, for better for worse, for richer for poorer, in sickness and in health, to love and to cherish, till death us do part, according to God's holy ordinance; and thereto I plight thee my troth.

SONIA: I, Sonia Mary Brownell, take thee, Eric, to be my wedded husband, to have and to hold from this day forward, for better for worse, for richer for poorer, in sickness and in health, to love and to cherish till death us do part, according to God's holy ordinance; and therefore I plight thee my troth.

ORWELL places a ring on SONIA's finger.

ORWELL: With this ring I thee wed, with my body I thee worship, and with my worldly goods I thee endow: In the name of the Father, and of the Son, and of the Holy Ghost. Amen.

SFX: Edmundo Ros 'Wedding Samba'.

ORWELL, still in his red velvet jacket, sits in an easy chair next to WARBURG, a pot of tea and some specification sheets near at hand.

Some people say that this BMB is the best light tractor you can buy, but I like the look of the Iron Horse. It seems more solidly constructed, which would help when it comes to cutting the hay, and even the oats come to that. It also has a 5 cwt trailer, which would be useful for potatoes, manure and so on. But can you run a dynamo off it? I mean, the Tilley lamps are serviceable, but I'm not sure Sonia would approve.

WARBURG: Sonia?

ORWELL: Yes, Sonia.

WARBURG: You're not taking Sonia to Jura?

ORWELL: I am.

WARBURG: But Sonia's not cut out for that sort of life.

ORWELL: I don't see why not.

SONIA enters.

Ah, there you are, darling. Just telling Warburg about our new tractor.

SONIA: Well, the tractor looks very nice, dear.

WARBURG stands as if to leave, remembers something.

WARBURG: Did you come up with anything?

ORWELL: What?

WARBURG: For Richard. I said I'd get him something for Christmas.

ORWELL: Oh yes, of course. Can one still get Meccano? Sonia, do you know?

SONIA: Meccano?

ORWELL: Yes. He's the right age for the simpler grades and he likes all those mechanical things.

WARBURG: I'll take a look in Hamley's, shall I?

SONIA: Hamley's?

ORWELL: It's a toy shop, darling.

WARBURG exits, walks down corridor, leaving ORWELL alone with SONIA who walks across to the window, folds her arms, turns.

SONIA: How old is Richard now anyway?

ORWELL: Five.

SONIA: And what are you going to do with him?

ORWELL: I really don't know. I can't cuddle him, you see, because of the danger of infection and I'm worried he'll grow away from me. And of course he misses his mother.

She was devoted to the boy and wanted to bring him up in the country, once the war was over, you know.

SONIA: Tell me about Eileen.

ORWELL: You knew Eileen.

SONIA: I didn't know Eileen.

ORWELL: You met her.

SONIA: Did I? I don't recall ever chatting to her. Did you love her?

ORWELL: Well, it wasn't perfect, but Eileen was a good old stick.

SONIA: A good old stick! I hope you won't talk about me that way.

ORWELL: Well, she was very different to you.

SONIA: In what way was she different, George?

ORWELL: Well, she didn't wear makeup or anything.

SONIA: Do I wear too much? Is that what you're saying?

ORWELL: No, of course not.

SONIA: How did she die? You've never told me.

ORWELL: In hospital. During an operation.

SONIA: For what?

ORWELL: A growth. Several growths in fact. She was in for a hysterectomy. She should have seen a specialist sooner, but I'd made a fuss about the money. There was no National Health, remember, and we couldn't get the really cheap rates because I made five hundred a year.

SONIA: She had cancer, didn't she?

ORWELL: Yes, she did. But she put the operation off in case it held up the adoption. We were old to be parents, you see, and she was simply terrified they'd find out she'd six months to live or something. So talk of cancer was out of the question. She would only talk about growths, and how much they cost to have removed. That's why she wanted me out of the way, so that when I came back she'd be convalescent.

SONIA: You left her in the lurch, didn't you?

ORWELL: I didn't know she was critical.

SONIA: But she was your wife. You're not blind, are you? I don't think you loved her at all.

ORWELL: Well, that's where you're wrong. I mean, we'd been through a lot together, and she understood all about my work.

SONIA: And work comes first with you, doesn't it?

ORWELL: Yes.

SONIA: I see it all so clearly now.

ORWELL: What?

SONIA: Your wife has growths in her uterus, she's bleeding and tired. You, meantime, refuse to cough up the money to make her better, and sleep with anyone who will have you.

ORWELL: Oh, I don't care much who sleeps with whom.

SONIA: You don't believe in fidelity?

ORWELL: No.

SONIA: Well, I shall remember that.

ORWELL: Where are you going?

SONIA: It's alright for you, George, lying here waited on hand and foot, but I've got others to minister to.

ORWELL: Who?

SONIA: Connolly.

ORWELL: What's wrong with him now?

SONIA: We're preparing the last edition and the whole place is falling apart.

Light source from the window changes to denote the passage of time.

SFX: Sound mix of printing press/news vendor/'The Radio Critics'.

ORWELL is sitting up in bed while FREUD draws him.

FREUD: So the wedding was right here in this room?

ORWELL: Yes.

FREUD: It all sounds very precipitous.

ORWELL: Well, Sonia was keen to crack on.

FREUD: Yes, Sonia can be very determined. And what did you do afterwards?

ORWELL: Nothing. The others went off to the Ritz Hotel. They all signed the menu, look.

ORWELL hands FREUD the signed menu.

I can't tell you how much it cost, what with the vintage champagne and all that.

FREUD: Did she come back afterwards?

ORWELL: And pretty tipsy I can tell you.

FREUD continues with his drawing, the only sound that of pencil on paper.

Haven't seen you for a while.

FREUD: I've been in Ireland

ORWELL: Enjoy it?

FREUD: Not really. I haven't been able to work, you see.

ORWELL: Writer's block sort of thing?

FREUD: No, I damaged my hand.

ORWELL: How?

FREUD: I punched Randolph Churchill in the face.

ORWELL: Oh, jolly well done.

FREUD: I must have hit him pretty hard because I couldn't hold a pencil for weeks. That's why I went away to Ireland. But I'd really like to get right away. To Morocco or somewhere like that. Trouble is, with these travel restrictions, no one can go anywhere. You were in Burma for a bit, weren't you?

ORWELL: Yes, I was stationed in Mandalay.

FREUD: And is Mandalay an exciting place?

ORWELL: No, very disagreeable.

FREUD: Why?

ORWELL: It has five main products all of which begin with P –
pagodas, pariahs, pigs, priests and prostitutes.

FREUD: Tell me about the prostitutes.

ORWELL: 'When I was young and had no sense / In far off
Mandalay / I lost my heart to a Burmese girl / As lovely as
the day.' Have you ever had a Burmese girl?

FREUD: No.

ORWELL: They have the most distinctive smell. It's a smell that
makes your teeth tingle.

FREUD: And what else did you like about the East?

ORWELL: Aside from the girls?

FREUD: Yes.

ORWELL: The palms and the blood-red hibiscus, the smell of
garlic in the air and the creaking of the ox cart wheels.

FREUD: Sounds very exotic.

ORWELL: But after a while you'd swop the whole lot for the sight
of a single daffodil, or a frozen pond, or a red pillar box.
And because the social life is so rank you sit night after night
in the Club, whisky to the right of you, pink 'un to the left,
listening to some old colonial telling you why the natives
should be boiled in oil. Worst of all is what happens to you.

FREUD: And what's that?

ORWELL: Well, one part of you starts to burn with a hatred of
your fellow countrymen and long for a native uprising to
drown the Empire in blood. The other part thinks that the
greatest joy in the world would be to drive a bayonet into
a Buddhist priest's guts. I came home with an immense
sense of guilt and did my damndest to get out of the system
altogether. Started spending my time with outcasts: beggars,
criminals, prostitutes. I wanted to escape, you see, not just
from imperialism but from every form of man's dominion
over his fellow man. Haven't you ever felt like that?

FREUD: I'm a Jewish refugee, George. I have no need of self-abasement.

ORWELL: Well, I had.

FREUD: And did it work?

ORWELL: I felt a sense of atonement, yes, and more than that, a sense of release which, looking back on it seems absurd, but which was vivid at the time.

FREUD: I don't know how you could lose your ambition.

ORWELL: Oh, I had ambition. I wanted to get put in prison.

FREUD: And did you succeed?

ORWELL: Only overnight.

FREUD: I've been in the police cells a few times.

ORWELL: What for?

FREUD: Fighting mostly.

FREUD draws with renewed vigour.

I owe a lot of money, you see.

ORWELL: How much do you need?

FREUD: Enough to pay off a gambling debt.

ORWELL: Well, sort something out with Sonia, will you? She seems to hold the purse strings these days.

FREUD, who has been drawing intently throughout this exchange, stands up abruptly.

FREUD: I think it's finished.

ORWELL: Can I see?

FREUD shows ORWELL the finished result.

Well, it has an unflinching realism.

FREUD: Yes, if there were a movement called 'Unflinching Realism', I would be the head of it.

ORWELL: Have you read the 'Story of Dorian Gray?'

FREUD: I have, yes.

ORWELL: And do you think human depravity manifests itself in the face?

FREUD: I haven't a clue.

ORWELL: Because this drawing shows a soul in pain.

FREUD: Yes, it does.

ORWELL: But I think it comes not so much from the pain you see in me as from the pain within yourself.

FREUD: Yes, I like to disturb myself.

ORWELL: And have you succeeded?

FREUD: Yes, I have.

ORWELL: Well, I think it's marvellous. May I have it?

FREUD: Yes, of course.

FREUD gives ORWELL the drawing and puts on the fur-collared great coat that's hanging on the back of the door.

Oh, hello Sonia.

SONIA sweeps past him brandishing copies of 'Horizon'.

SONIA hands a copy each to ORWELL and FREUD.

SONIA: We wanted to put out a bumper edition, but needless to say the printer jibbed.

ORWELL glances at the table of contents.

ORWELL: Who's Norman Mailer?

SONIA: The coming man.

ORWELL: Really?

SONIA: In fact, I'd go so far as to say that 'The Naked and the Dead' is the most scrupulously honest war novel ever published.

FREUD: Yes, that's what it says in here.

SONIA tries to snatch the copy of 'Horizon' from FREUD, but FREUD hangs on to it and continues thumbing through it.

NURSE enters with wheelchair.

SONIA: What's that for?

NURSE: Mr Orwell is going for his X-ray.

SONIA. Then I shall come too.

NURSE: I'm afraid that's strictly forbidden, Miss Brownell, I beg your pardon, Mrs Orwell.

SONIA: Well, how long is he going to be? I mean, is it worth my while hanging round?

NURSE: Oh, we'll have him back in no time at all.

SONIA: Then I shall wait.

NURSE helps ORWELL into wheelchair and pushes it, squeaking, out of the room and into the corridor, leaving SONIA and FREUD alone in Room 65.

FREUD: I don't understand why you married him.

SONIA: No, neither do I. I'm hardly the Ministering Angel type, am I?

FREUD: No.

SONIA: Well, you might have hesitated a bit.

FREUD: And who is it you think you've married?

SONIA: That is a ridiculous question.

FREUD: On the door it says Eric Blair. Did you marry Eric Blair? Or did you marry a man called George Orwell?

SONIA: What makes you say that?

FREUD: I think Orwell is a mask worn by Blair.

SONIA: You're quite the little psychiatrist, aren't you?

FREUD: Well, you know, it runs in the family.

SONIA: So tell me why he married me.

FREUD: He thinks he's repulsive.

SONIA: Utter claptrap.

FREUD: You, Sonia, are a dream to him. You represent this beautiful woman he's thought about all his life and never been able to have. Until now.

SONIA: And why did I marry him?

FREUD: Because being the wife of a man of letters gives you status, instant status. You'll have a share of his literary fame, you'll have security, independence. You'll have to live without love, of course. Without sex. Without passion. Will you be able to do that?

SONIA: Love and passion, Lucian, have brought me only unhappiness.

FREUD: Well, I could never get married again.

SONIA: Why?

FREUD: Because when I start to love someone she becomes my mother and I could never make love to my mother.

SONIA picks up the drawing of ORWELL and examines it closely.

SONIA: This is truly horrible.

FREUD: You think so?

SONIA: Yes.

FREUD tears the drawing into pieces and drops them on the floor.

SONIA starts to pick up the pieces of paper, an action which brings her to her knees in front of FREUD.

FREUD: He said you were to lend me some money.

SONIA: And why on earth would I do that?

FREUD: Your husband says you control the purse strings. Do you control the purse stings?

SONIA: No.

FREUD: Then why would George tell me you did?

SONIA: How much do you want anyway?

FREUD: Three thousand pounds.

SONIA: Three thousand pounds!

FREUD: Yes, three thousand pounds.

SONIA: How much do you think Cyril pays me?

FREUD: I don't know.

SONIA: Thirty bob a week.

FREUD: Plus lunch at the White Tower everyday.

SONIA: No, not every day. Sometimes we go to the Cafe Royale. And why do you need £3,000?

FREUD: Because if I don't give them £3,000 they'll cut my hand off. Or my tongue.

SONIA: What is this? A gambling debt?

FREUD: Yes.

SONIA: But how could you lose £3,000?

FREUD: I like living dangerously.

SONIA: You're not still pulling that stupid stunt of shutting your eyes and dashing across the road, are you?

FREUD: Yes. How else would I know I was alive?

SONIA: What's Simone de Beauvoir like?

FREUD: In bed?

SONIA: Yes.

FREUD: Too serious.

SONIA: She's competing with Sartre, you know.

FREUD: To be serious?

SONIA: No, to fuck the most people. Why do you do it?

FREUD: What?

SONIA: You know, gamble.

FREUD: I like to lose. It makes me feel alive. Like sex.

SONIA: Sex?

FREUD: Yes, sex. Now where did you consummate your marriage. Here? On the bed? In that chair? On the floor? Or did you do it standing up? Can George stand up? Can George get it up? Well, so far as I'm concerned, you're not really married anyway.

SONIA: I certainly am.

FREUD: But marriage to a bed-ridden man is as near to no marriage as one can get. I actually don't know how you can touch him. I mean, with that smell of decay on him.

SONIA: Oh, I'm getting used to the smell.

FREUD: What is it?

SONIA: His lungs. It's his rotting lungs

FREUD: Do you make love?

SONIA: No, of course we don't. How can you ask such a stupid thing? I mean, you can see how ill he is.

FREUD reaches out a hand to her. SONIA pulls away. FREUD closes the door.

SONIA: Get away from me.

FREUD: What's that you're wearing? That scent, what is it?

SONIA: It's called 'Forbidden'.

FREUD: I hate women who smell of scent. Women should smell of one thing only.

SONIA: What's that?

FREUD: Cunt.

SONIA: You really are a creep, aren't you?

FREUD grabs her.

Oh, don't be so ridiculous. I mean here? Of all places.

FREUD: But that's what makes it so exciting.

SONIA: But anyone passing the door can see us.

FREUD hangs his coat on the back of the door obliterating the porthole and approaches SONIA.

And what do you smell of? Oh yes, paint and turpentine.

FREUD kisses her.

You are quite mad.

FREUD: Yes, probably.

SONIA: I mean, think of the risk.

FREUD: I like the risk.

SONIA: Anyone could come in.

FREUD: Yes, I know.

SONIA: I must be corrupt to my very bones.

They make frantic and quite noisy love.

WARBURG walks downstage along the hospital corridor and is about to open the door to Room 65 when he hears the sound of love-making from within.

He takes a step back and sees, approaching behind him, ORWELL being pushed by the NURSE in a wheelchair.

WARBURG opens the door of Room 65 and, without going in, bangs it shut, then turns back to waylay the approaching ORWELL.

WARBURG: Hello, George.

ORWELL: Fred, what are you doing here?

WARBURG: I just wanted to go through that list.

ORWELL: List?

WARBURG goes into his inside pocket and produces a folded sheet of paper.

WARBURG: See if you want to add anything.

ORWELL: Right.

WARBURG: I've got marrow jam.

ORWELL: What?

WARBURG: Marrow jam.

ORWELL: Yes, I like marrow jam.

WARBURG: Well, that's why I've got it on the list. I've also put down gentleman's relish, kippers, stilton and saffron buns. How are you off for marmalade?

ORWELL looks up towards the nurse.

NURSE: It's the…

WARBURG: Cooper's Oxford, yes, I know.

ORWELL: Got something on your mind, have you, Fred?

WARBURG: No, I don't think so.

ORWELL: Want to come in and have a chat?

WARBURG: I'm meeting Alberto Moravia. Have you read his 'Woman of Rome'…?

As WARBURG maunders on, FREUD and SONIA continue to make themselves look presentable.

It isn't great art of course, but stories about prostitutes always do well. I mean, it's very far from obscene, and publishers have to eat, after all.

SONIA, opens the door of Room 65.

SONIA: George, where on earth have you been?

ORWELL: For an X-ray.

SONIA: Well, I know that! But how on earth can it take so long? I've been hanging around here for hours.

ORWELL: We were less than 20 minutes.

LUCIAN FREUD pokes his head out of the door.

Oh, hello, Lucian. You still here?

SONIA: He was showing me his drawing.

ORWELL: Good. Jolly good.

SONIA: I'll take him, nurse.

NURSE: We're short of wheelchairs.

SONIA: Well, you'll have to come back for it, won't you?

NURSE exits upstage along the corridor.

WARBURG: I'll say goodbye then.

ORWELL: Yes, and thank you so much for coming in.

WARBURG: Good luck, George. With everything.

ORWELL: Thank you, Fred.

WARBURG exits upstage.

Salt of the earth, that Warburg fellow.

FREUD pushes the wheelchair into Room 65 and helps ORWELL into an easy chair.

I hope those X-rays turn out okay.

SONIA: Of course they will, George, of course they will.

FREUD and SONIA exchange glances as they try to cover their tracks by kicking bits of the drawing under the bed.

Light from the window changes to indicate the passage of time.

SFX: Sound mix of charladies scrubbing floor/man whistling in corridor/'Workers' Playtime' radio show.

ORWELL and SONIA sit in chairs in Room 65.

ORWELL, much to SONIA's annoyance, is drinking tea from a saucer.

It's been a bit of a whirl, hasn't it?

ORWELL: What?

SONIA: Getting married in such haste.

ORWELL: You're not repenting already, are you?

SONIA: No, not at all, you silly old thing. But there's so much I don't know about you. I mean, what's your routine?

ORWELL: When I'm well, you mean?

SONIA: Yes.

ORWELL: Well, every day at quarter to eight Richard wakes me by tickling my feet. I have to be woken gently, you see, because I have the most terrible nightmares.

SONIA: You don't shout out in your sleep, do you?

ORWELL: Yes, and sometimes I scream. Then at half past eight Richard and I have breakfast together and each day I make the same little joke of putting a tea cloth over my arm and pretending to be a waiter. Richard finds that terribly funny. Then I start work and keep going to lunch time when, if I'm not meeting someone, I go to the pub and have a sandwich. Then, in the afternoon I'll potter about a bit or I might do some carpentry. Then Richard and I will eat high tea. We're both very fond of semolina pudding flavoured with lemon and vanilla. Can you make that?

SONIA shakes her head.

Then I'll play with him for half an hour, put him to bed and go back to work until ten o'clock sharp when I always have cocoa in a Victorian Jubilee mug. Cadbury's cocoa for preference, but if I can't find any in the shops I'll settle for Fry's, though I find Fry's a very poor second best. I'm very particular about milk. It has to be almost on the boil and frothing before the chocolate is added and stirred with a wooden spoon, it has to be a wooden spoon. Then I go back to work and keep going until about three in the morning.

SONIA: And where shall we do this?

ORWELL: If I recover really well I should like to move back to Jura.

SONIA: I think you need a healthier climate.

ORWELL: But Jura has an unbeatable climate. Gulf Stream and all that, you know. You hardly ever get frost or snow. It rains all the time of course, but after a while one gets used to that.

SONIA: But Jura is where you got ill.

ORWELL: Oh, that was nothing to do with Jura. I got ill in Canonbury Square during the winter of '47 when we had all the power cuts. Look, this is Barnhill.

ORWELL rummages through a drawer and produces a photograph.

SONIA: It's very remote.

ORWELL: Well, that's the whole point. If they drop an atom bomb on Glasgow there will be only two tidal waves and Jura will survive unscathed.

SONIA: How do you know that?

ORWELL: I've done my research.

SONIA: But how do you get to a place like this?

ORWELL: Well, you get the train to Glasgow, bus to the west coast, boat to Kintyre, bus across Kintyre, boat to Jura and taxi from Craighouse to Ardlussa.

SONIA: And you're there?

ORWELL: No. The last five miles is a rutted cart-track. You have to take that on foot, though we have a horse for emergencies.

SONIA: And how long does this ordeal take?

ORWELL: About 48 hours.

SONIA: You can be half way round the world in that time.

ORWELL: You wouldn't be in Jura though, would you?

SONIA: Can you stop doing that?

ORWELL: Doing what?

SONIA: Slurping your tea from the saucer like that.

ORWELL: I didn't know it upset you.

SONIA: Well, it does. You're not in the doss house now, you know, George.

ORWELL: Oh.

SONIA: So where do you buy your food and stuff?

ORWELL: At the general store in Craighouse.

SONIA: And how far is Craighouse?

ORWELL: 25 miles. Craighouse is where the steamers come in.

SONIA: And where's the nearest telephone?

ORWELL: About 15 miles away.

SONIA looks at the photograph of Barnhill.

SONIA: But George, this is bleak.

ORWELL: It isn't bleak. There's only a field between us and the sea and on the other side of the island there's an empty shepherd's hut where you can sleep next to endless white sands.

SONIA: But how do you get about the place?

ORWELL: Well, I tend to travel by motorbike.

SONIA: And what do you eat?

ORWELL: Well, the lochs are simply teeming with trout because there's nobody there to fish them. There's venison, rabbit, lobster, mackerel. And I've started making this carrageen pudding.

SONIA: What's carrageen pudding?

ORWELL: Well, you go down to the seashore and pick up the seaweed, the carrageen, then you peg it out to dry, then you stew it.

SONIA: It sounds disgusting.

ORWELL: Yes, it is, it's absolutely disgusting. But edible, quite edible.

SONIA: And how do you occupy your time? When you're not collecting carrageen.

ORWELL: By writing, of course.

SONIA: But when you're not writing?

ORWELL: I help out with the hay-making, I search for lost hens, I fish, I shoot rabbits.

NURSE appears at the porthole outside Room 65 and looks in before opening the door and entering.

NURSE: And how is the patient feeling this evening?

ORWELL: I seem to have perked up a bit.

NURSE: And physically?

ORWELL: Still coughing away like billyo, and I seem to have cold feet all the time.

NURSE: Yes, that's quite common with TB.

ORWELL: Really?

NURSE: I know D. H. Lawrence had cold feet because Mr Morland told me so. But his wife, so it's said, was a tower of strength.

SONIA: Why, what did she do?

NURSE: She warmed his feet.

SONIA: How?

NURSE is unsure whether to reveal the next piece of information, but eventually decides to do so.

NURSE: Well, she had a the most splendid bosom. That always seemed to do the trick.

SONIA: Yes, I don't doubt it.

NURSE: In any event, I have good news. Mr Morland has seen your X-rays and says your tubercles are no worse. If anything, they're in abeyance.

SONIA: Oh, George, did you hear that? In abeyance.

NURSE: It's not a clean bill of health, of course, but combined with your feeling rather better, Mr Morland suggests a stay in a sanitorium.

ORWELL: Where?

NURSE: He favours one outside Gstaad in a place called Montana Vermala.

ORWELL: You're saying I can get out of here?

NURSE: Yes.

SONIA and ORWELL embrace.

SONIA: Oh, George, that is the most wonderful news.

ORWELL: Well, I think this calls for a celebration. Will you join us?

NURSE: Not while I'm on duty, no. But I am very pleased for you. Very pleased for both of you.

NURSE exits, SONIA pours two very large whiskies.

SONIA: My God, George, what a relief.

They chink glasses.

ORWELL: Your very good health.

They drink, SONIA very quickly, before a refill.

SONIA: Are your feet still cold, George?

ORWELL: Yes.

SONIA goes to the foot of the bed, takes off her jumper, blouse and brassiere.

Now what are you up to?

SONIA: Well, if D. H. Lawrence can have his feet warmed, so can George Orwell.

SONIA cups ORWELL's feet in her breasts.

ORWELL: Oh, what I'd do to you if I were able.

SONIA: What would you do, George? What would you do?

ORWELL: I'd tie you naked to a stake and shoot you full of arrows.

SONIA: What then?

ORWELL: I'd ravish you.

SONIA: Really?

ORWELL: Yes. And then at the moment of climax I'd cut your throat.

Light from the window again indicates the passage of time.

SFX: Sound mix of Third Programme/railway porter/Charlie Chester.

WARBURG, SONIA and ORWELL sit at an improvised 'office' space in Room 65.

WARBURG opens his briefcase and produces a document.

WARBURG: I now call to order this meeting of George Orwell Productions. Those present, Mr Fredric Warburg, Mr Eric Blair and Mrs Eric Blair…

SONIA: Sonia Orwell.

WARBURG: For the purpose of this meeting, Sonia, you are Mrs Eric Blair.

SONIA: Well, I hate being Mrs Eric Blair.

WARBURG: You are married to Mr Eric Blair. Hence, you are Mrs Eric Blair. Now may we proceed?

SONIA: Yes, if you must.

WARBURG: Apologies for absence from Mr Jack Harrison.

SONIA: I've never heard of Jack Harrison.

WARBURG: He's senior partner at Harrison Hill.

SONIA: And what's Harrison Hill?

ORWELL: A firm of Chartered Accountants, dear.

SONIA: So where is he?

WARBURG: His presence is neither here nor there because I hold his proxy vote.

SONIA: And what is it we're voting on?

WARBURG: Whether to give Mrs Eric Blair a place on the board and a share in the company.

SONIA: Oh.

WARBURG: All those in favour say Aye. Aye.

ORWELL: Aye.

WARBURG: Congratulations, Sonia, you are now a partner in George Orwell Productions. Just sign here.

SONIA: But why am I doing this?

ORWELL: It's the tax.

SONIA: The tax?

WARBURG: Yes, the tax.

SONIA: Why the tax?

WARBURG: Well, let's just put it this way, Sonia – were George to make £3,000 a year he would pay half of that in tax.

SONIA: That's absolutely scandalous.

WARBURG: Yes, but once you earn that kind of money you pay ten shillings in the pound. That's 50%.

SONIA: I know what it is, Fred, I'm not stupid.

WARBURG: And now things are going from bad to worse.

SONIA: Why?

WARBURG: Well, George and I are keen on this film deal.

SONIA: What film deal?

WARBURG: For 'Animal Farm'.

SONIA: I know nothing of this.

WARBURG: I've been keeping it under wraps, but last week we received a firm offer.

SONIA: From who?

WARBURG: MGM.

SONIA: George, what are you thinking of?

ORWELL: Reaches a lot of people, film.

WARBURG: The point is, if we go ahead, George will be liable to surtax.

SONIA: What's surtax?

WARBURG: Well, it's even more.

SONIA: But how much more?

WARBURG: The top rate is 95%.

SONIA: That can't be true.

WARBURG: I'm afraid it is. But, naturally, as George's publisher and business adviser, I have matters in hand. Now if you'll sign where I've indicated. Here, here, and again here.

SONIA signs. WARBURG puts the top on the pen.

There, you are now a partner in George Orwell Productions.

SONIA: But what does that mean?

WARBURG: It means that taxable income from George's published work will in future be paid to the Company and that you, as a shareholder, will be entitled to a percentage of the proceeds.

SONIA: But what percentage?

WARBURG: An equal share.

SONIA: With whom?

WARBURG: With George. And I, though to a lesser degree, a much lesser degree. Now I must be off, I'm having lunch with Thomas Mann.

ORWELL: How is the old fake?

WARBURG: Obsessed with Schonberg.

WARBURG puts on homburg, exits.

ORWELL: Well, I don't think there's an answer to that. You haven't seen my drawing, have you?

SONIA: What drawing?

ORWELL: That one of Freud's.

SONIA: Oh, I took it back to Percy Street.

ORWELL: Why?

SONIA: To have something to remind me of you.

She goes over and kisses him.

ORWELL: I can't wait to get out of here.

SONIA: I'm in two minds about Switzerland.

ORWELL: Why?

SONIA: Well, I'm not a nurse.

ORWELL: It's a clinic, Sonia. The place will be overrun with nurses.

SONIA: But how am I to get you there? I mean, on my own?

ORWELL: I've no idea, but people must have done it before.

SONIA: But have you thought how much it will cost? I mean, you could be there for months.

ORWELL: Don't worry about money, Sonia. There's this Book-of-the-Month Club deal. And the film.

SONIA: Yes, the film. I don't think you should do it, George.

ORWELL: Why ever not?

SONIA: Because you can't trust those kind of people.

ORWELL: What kind of people?

SONIA: Those Hollywood types.

ORWELL: I'll make sure they follow the story line.

SONIA: Have you seen 'The Grapes of Wrath'?

ORWELL: Yes, I reviewed it.

SONIA: Well, look what a horse's arse that turned out.

SONIA takes herself off to the window and gazes out.

Have you ever been to Neuchâtel?

ORWELL: No.

SONIA: When I was 17, I was packed off to stay with a family there. They had a daughter called Madeleine, and one day two boys took us sailing. Then, as we tacked back across the lake, the sky turned black and this squall blew up. I mean, it just came out of the blue and in seconds the boat capsized. Well, I was the only one who could swim. They couldn't, you see, they couldn't swim, God knows what they were doing in a boat. Anyway, there they were, the two boys clinging on to the boat and holding Madeleine up between them. Well, I swam back to help them of course, but one by one they all went under. Then one of the boys grabbed hold of me. I mean, he held me really tight, like a drowning man, which is what he was. He wanted to drag me down with him, I mean he was fighting for his life, and so was I. So I grabbed him by the hair and pushed his head under the water. I held him down for a few seconds, then let go. I thought he'd stop fighting me, you see, and come back up to the surface. He didn't.

ORWELL: But you can't blame yourself for that.

SONIA: I killed him, George. That's why I'm not keen on Switzerland.

Light source from the window again indicates the passage of time.

SFX: Sound mix made up of hospital trolleys/the Hokey Cokey/ errand boy.

ORWELL, dressed in corduroy trousers, dark blue shirt, tweed jacket, is assembling a fishing rod.

FRED WARBURG, at his side, is reading a newspaper.

A pair of size 12 boots stand nearby on the floor.

WARBURG: Have you heard of a bloke called Tom Braddock?

ORWELL: No.

WARBURG: Labour MP apparently.

ORWELL: And what's he got to say for himself?

WARBURG: 'The workers of this country have agreed that they want for themselves all they produce, all the wealth of the country, all the food, all the housing, all the clothing. Their legitimate needs can only be met by all: there is no surplus for the cultured few, for the royal and noble few, for the wealthy few. All these must be stripped of their rents, of their interest, of their profit and of their inflated salaries and expense accounts.'

'Chuck it comrades,' he says, 'be workers and be proud of it, be rough, be unreasonable, don't worship slick efficiency. It is the workers who are important, not the work, the work is secondary.'

ORWELL: Hmm.

WARBURG: Well, what do you think?

ORWELL picks up the pair of boots.

ORWELL: I can't thank you enough for these. They're just the thing for hill walking.

WARBURG: You don't want to exert yourself, George.

ORWELL weighs the boots in his hands, anticipating the pleasure with which he will wear them.

He puts the boots back on the floor, then picks one up and polishes the toe-cap with his sleeve.

ORWELL: Think I'm too old for corduroy?

WARBURG: What's that?

ORWELL: Corduroy. Sonia says I'm too old for it.

WARBURG: The fish won't mind much what you wear.

ORWELL: I was thinking more about evening wear. In the sanitorium.

WARBURG: Right.

ORWELL: Sonia likes the idea of blue serge. Would blue serge be appropriate?

WARBURG: Don't see why not.

He makes some practice casts.

ORWELL: Some people don't get fishing, do they? But it's not a thing you can rationalise. It's magic, a sort of fairy light that fish and fishing bring to me. I mean, sitting all day beside a quiet pool belongs to a time before the war, before radio, before aeroplanes, before the bomb. There's even a kind of peacefulness in the names of English fish. Roach, rudd, barbel, bream, gudgeon, pike, chub, carp, tench. The people who made those names up didn't spend their time going to the pictures and wondering when someone would drop the bomb.

Light source from the window changes to indicate the passage of time.

SFX: Sound design of reel being cast/birdsong/angler's chat.

SONIA sits with ORWELL. He hands her a legal document.

I've drawn up a new will.

SONIA: And what does it say?

ORWELL: It names you as the sole beneficiary. But I've made a request that, when you write a will, you leave what's left to Richard. Is that alright?

SONIA: Yes, of course it is.

ORWELL: You'll also see, if you read on, that I've made you my literary executor.

SONIA: Well, I'm very touched.

ORWELL: And you'll make sure nothing gets mucked about?

SONIA: Well, of course I will.

ORWELL: And I want no biography.

SONIA: No biography. I'll see to it. Oh, don't look so worried, George, I'll take care of everything.

ORWELL: I know you will, darling. But I'm concerned about this trip.

SONIA: Why?

ORWELL: I don't think I'm up to the train journey.

SONIA: Of course you're not, and that's why we'll fly.

ORWELL: Isn't that just as bothersome?

SONIA: Not if we go by private charter.

ORWELL: Private charter?

SONIA: Straight by car to Croydon Airport, step on the plane and bob's your uncle. The whole thing will be a piece of cake. And Lucian will be there to help.

ORWELL: Lucian?

SONIA: Yes, Lucian. You like Lucian, don't you?

ORWELL: Yes, but…

SONIA: I'll take the wheelchair, and he'll do the lifting and carrying.

ORWELL: But why does he want to tag along?

SONIA: Oh, he's desperate to get out of London and sample a bit of mountain air. It's really very good of him, offering to help like this.

ORWELL: So it'll be just the three of us?

SONIA: Well, I won't be able to stay with you, and I can't be on my own all day, can I?

ORWELL: No, of course not.

SONIA: It's not like there's tons to do in Gstaad, and we're not even in Gstaad. We're somewhere called Montana Vermala. I mean, what will I do all day? Yodle?

ORWELL: No.

SONIA: So Lucian will help me pass the time. Besides, I don't suppose he'll stay long, what with Anne Dunn on the scene.

ORWELL: But how much is the aeroplane?

SONIA: I've no idea, but Fred says money isn't a problem, and it's your health we're thinking of.

ORWELL: Mmm.

SONIA: Oh, don't worry, it'll be fine.

ORWELL: But what about tea?

SONIA: What?

ORWELL: Tea. The Swiss drink that filthy Chinese stuff. I like Ceylon tea, very strong.

SONIA: I'll make sure we take plenty with us, George.

ORWELL: You are so very good to me, Sonia.

SONIA: Now you see you get a good night's sleep.

ORWELL: And what are you up to?

SONIA: Early night. We've got a big day tomorrow, George.

She kisses him on the forehead, exits.

Light source from the window indicates passage of time.

SFX: Night club/corks popping/drunken chatter.

The night of Jan 21st. ORWELL in bed. A blood vessel ruptures in his lung. No one hears his strangled cries for help, he is unable to reach the emergency bell and he dies at once and alone.

SFX: Phone rings and rings endlessly.

SONIA, in cocktail dress, runs downstage, followed by FREUD and protesting NURSE.

NURSE: We've been calling and calling all night long.

SONIA enters Room 65 where the empty bed is still covered in bloody sheets.

SONIA puts a hand on the bed, picks up an end of the bloodied sheet and slowly wraps it round herself before falling to her knees, prostrate with grief.

FREUD and NURSE, in the corridor, look on in silence.

Light source from the window indicates passage of time.

SFX: Radio.

ANNOUNCER: Here is the news for today the 22nd of January. The death occurred last night of Mr George Orwell, the author, at the age of 46. He had been ill for a long time.

George Orwell was educated at Eton and later served in the Burma police. He fought on the Republican side in the Spanish Civil War and was wounded. He will, perhaps, be best remembered for 'Animal Farm', a satire on life in the Soviet Union, and for the recently published '1984', a grim imaginary picture of a totalitarian Great Britain some 30 years from now, which was highly praised by critics on both sides of the Atlantic.

SONIA walks down the hospital corridor and turns into Room 65 where the bloodied sheets have been stripped from the bed.

She takes ORWELL's clothes from the wardrobe and cupboards and folds them neatly on the bed.

Then she starts to go through the drawers, glancing through various personal items, including some McGill postcards.

WARBURG appears at the door.

SONIA: Oh, hello Fred, what are you doing here?

WARBURG: Thought I'd see if I could lend a hand.

SONIA: That's very considerate of you, Fred.

WARBURG: He told me he had an idea for a novel.

SONIA: 'A Smoking Room Story'.

WARBURG: Is it there? Even a story outline would do.

SONIA: Would do what?

WARBURG: Keep his memory alive.

SONIA: There's some of his silly postcards here. He liked a bit of vulgarity, George.

WARBURG: There will need to be a biography.

SONIA: No biography, Fred.

WARBURG: That isn't for you to decide, Sonia.

SONIA hands ORWELL the will from her handbag.

And when did this happen?

SONIA: Yesterday.

WARBURG: Did he say anything about the film? Because MGM are very keen.

SONIA: There will be no film.

WARBURG: But George was excited by the idea.

SONIA: Yes, but I'm not.

WARBURG: Tell me you'll at least talk to them.

SONIA: No.

WARBURG: Sonia, a talk, what harm can it do?

SONIA: This is very bad timing, Fred.

WARBURG: I know, and I apologise, but please hear me out.

SONIA sits down on the bed and gives WARBURG her attention.

You must remember, Sonia, that I have known George far longer than you. I mean, we were friends. I was his Corporal in the Home Guard. I published 'Homage to Catalonia', a book, by the way, that has, to this day, sold less than 500 copies. But did he bring me 'Animal Farm'? No, he did not! And do you know why? He thought me unsound, financially and politically. So he took the manuscript to the big boys. First to Cape, who turned it down on the grounds that it might offend the Soviets. Pah! Next he sent it to Faber & Faber, who returned it with a note saying that the pigs, as the most intelligent animals on the farm, were the most qualified to run it and that what was needed were more public-spirited pigs. More public-spirited pigs, I ask you! And who do you think penned that response? T. S. bloody Eliot, that's who. So next he tries his luck in the States. And what happens there? I'll tell you what happens. Dial Press write back to say there's no demand for animal stories. Moi vey! No demand for animal stories! So there I am, in a bar off the Strand, and in walks George. 'I've got something for you,' he says and hands me this dog-eared manuscript. 'What is it?' I ask. 'Read it', he says, 'though I don't suppose you'll like it much. It's about a lot of animals on a farm who rebel against the farmer and it's very anti-Russian. Much too anti-Russian for you'. 'What's it called?' I ask. 'It's called "Animal Farm"', he says and a few moments later he's gone. So I walk back to my office with the manuscript in my hand, not yet aware that I have received a gift more precious than rubies. That evening I read it and know at once it's a masterpiece. But, supposing I'd turned down 'Animal Farm', what do you think would have happened to George? A deep depression, even despair, might well have swept over him. Yes, he was a man of iron will, but he had much to endure in life, and in 1943 he was 40. How long did he have to complete his work? No, if 'Animal Farm' had failed, even his morale might have cracked.

WARBURG picks up a copy of ORWELL's '1984'.

And this book, Sonia, this wonderful book, would never have seen the light of day. It would have been found here among his papers, abandoned, unfinished, incomplete, and you, Sonia, would now destroy it in accordance with the instructions of this will.

As if to put the matter beyond doubt WARBURG waves ORWELL's will around the room.

The face of English literature in the twentieth century would have been unutterably changed. In July 1943, of course, none of this occurred to me. I was a small insignificant publisher, hard pressed for paper, my office wrecked by a flying bomb. But I had one overwhelming asset, a belief in your husband's work, a willingness to risk everything for him. That's why he put his faith in me. That's why he signed a contract for three more books. Three more books, Sonia. Three more books. Thus far I have only had one of them. But he was reckless of his health, and indeed his life, and now there will be no more books. Not even the biography the world is crying out for. Not even, yes I'll say it again, not even the film that George had set his heart on.

WARBURG puts his homburg on and turns to the door.

I'll see you at the funeral.

SONIA: Fred.

WARBURG: Yes.

SONIA: Who's the most famous film-star in the world?

WARBURG: I don't know, Sonia.

SONIA: I think it's Clark Gable.

WARBURG: You're probably right. Yes, I agree, it's Clark Gable.

SONIA: Well, tell them I want to meet Clark Gable.

WARBURG: I beg your pardon.

SONIA: Tell them I want to meet Clark Gable. Clark Gable is signed to MGM.

WARBURG: Is he?

SONIA: Yes, he is.

WARBURG: So what is it you want me to do?

SONIA: I want you to set up a meeting.

WARBURG: With you and Clark Gable?

SONIA: Yes, that's right.

WARBURG: And then you'll do the deal?

SONIA: I'll think about it. Oh, and Fred.

WARBURG: Yes.

SONIA: Don't forget the fishing rod.

WARBURG: You don't want it?

SONIA: Not where I'm going.

WARBURG: And where are you going?

SONIA: To the south of France, with Maurice.

WARBURG takes the fishing rod, exits. SONIA looks around the room and sees ORWELL's size 12 boots. She picks up one of the boots and puts her hand inside it to feel where ORWELL's feet would have been. She rubs the shoe against her cheek. She puts the boot down beside its partner, kicks off the shoes she's wearing, and puts the boots on.

She walks up and down in them, then turns in them sharply, each movement becoming more rhythmical.

SFX: Edmundo Ros 'Enjoy Yourself It's Later Than You Think'.

SONIA takes ORWELL's crimson smoking jacket off the bed and, taking her husband in her arms, dances out of the room and exits up the hospital corridor.

THE END